Authentic Traditional Pennsylvania Dutch Amish and Mennonite Recipes

Introduction	1
Amish Apple Butter	2
Amish Cup Cheese	3
Pennsylvania Dutch Scrapple	4
Mennonite Apple Dumplings	5
Amish Chow Chow	6
Pennsylvania Dutch Beet Eggs	7
Amish Cole Slaw	8
Amish Corn Soup with Rivels	9
Lancaster Amish Pretzels	10
Authentic Amish Potato Salad	12
Pennsylvania Dutch Meat Rolls	14
Pennsylvania Dutch Pot Pie	15
Browned Butter Noodles	17
Amish Corn Fritters	18
Schnitz Un Gnepp	19
Pennsylvania Dutch Sauerbraten	20
Mennonite Ham Loaf	22
Pennsylvania Dutch Potato Filling	23
Amish Friendship Bread	25
Amish Friendship Bread Starter	26
Amish Potato Rolls	28
Snickerdoodles	29
Amish Gingersnaps Cookies	30
Shoofly Pie	31
Whoopie pie	32

Introduction

The Amish and The Mennonites live in a large concentration in Lancaster, Pennsylvania. The cuisine of these groups is that of simple and traditional Americana with roots in German style cooking. Indeed they are often referred to as the Pennsylvania Dutch. Their food is important to their social life in the form of church socials, potlucks, wedding, fundraisers and other events.

The Amish and Mennonites were once one group all known as Mennonites. The more conservative group split and called themselves Amish or Amish-Mennonites. Today they still dress conservatively, work very hard with strong social and Christian religious beliefs but some groups allow for more modern conveniences such as automobiles and cell phones. Indeed, these groups own lots of businesses such as restaurants, furniture stores and contracting for houses. Where I live in Northern Baltimore County there are several of these businesses since Lancaster is about a twenty minute drive from my house. My house is filled with Amish-Mennonite made furniture and my cupboards are filled with Amish-Mennonite made preserves, pickled produce and canned goods. Being that Lancaster is so close, I have been there countless times and eaten at the restaurants and shopped at the stores. However, it isn't really necessary for me to drive to Lancaster to see the Amish or eat in one of their restaurants since there are several of these establishments right down the street from me.

I've talked to many Amish members and asked them what dishes that they considered true authentic and traditional Amish cuisine. This book contains the list of what they felt were the best dishes to represent their culture.

Amish Apple Butter

Ingredients:

12 cooking apples, (such as Granny Smith)
1 ½ cups packed brown sugar
½ cup apple juice
1 tbsp. ground cinnamon
1 tbsp. lemon juice
1 tsp. ground allspice
1 tsp. ground nutmeg
½ tsp. ground cloves

Directions:

1. Core, peel and cut apples in to fourths.
2. Mix all ingredients in a large slow cooker.
3. Cover and cook on low heat setting 8 to 10 hours or until apples are very tender.
4. Mash apples with potato masher or large fork.
5. Cook uncovered on low heat setting 1 to 2 hours, stirring occasionally, until mixture is very thick.
6. Cool about 2 hours.
7. Spoon apple butter into container.
8. Cover and store in refrigerator for up to 3 weeks.

Amish Cup Cheese

Ingredients:

2 1/2 gal fresh raw milk
1 1/2 tsp. baking soda
1 1/2 tsp. salt
1/2 cup water

Directions:

1. Let milk sour until it is very thick.
2. Heat to 120 degrees and pour into a coarse cloth bag.
3. Let it drain overnight.
4. Crumble curds until they are fine.
5. Mix soda with cheese thoroughly.
6. Place in a medium bowl, cover with a cloth and let set at room temperature for 3 days.
7. Stir every morning and evening.
8. At the end of the third day, place the bowl of cheese in the upper part of a double boiler.
9. Over heat, stir in salt and water until smooth.
10. Cheese should be thick and yellow and have a sharp smell.
11. Pour into cup sized containers.
12. Let cool.
13. Spread on bread to serve.

Pennsylvania Dutch Scrapple

Ingredients:

1 ½ lb. ground pork
5 cups water, divided
1 tsp. salt
½ tsp. sage
1 cup cornmeal

Directions:

1. Break up the ground pork into small pieces in a large saucepan.
2. Add 4 cups of water and stir, separating the pork well.
3. Heat to boiling, reduce to simmer and cook 30 minutes.
4. Remove meat from stock.
5. Reserve 3 cups of the stock.
6. Add salt and sage to the stock.
7. Combine the cornmeal with 1 cup cold water.
8. Add the cornmeal mixture gradually to the hot stock.
9. Bring to a boil then reduce to simmer.
10. Cover, and cook for 15 minutes.
11. Stir in cooked ground pork.
12. Pour into a loaf pan (9 ½ x 5 x 3 inches).
13. Chill for 24 hours.
14. Slice ¼- to ½-inch thick.
15. Fry pieces in hot oil quickly, turning only once.
16. Serve and enjoy!

Note: Good with syrup!

Mennonite Apple Dumplings

Ingredients:

1/2 cup water
1/4 cup granulated sugar
1 teaspoon vanilla extract
2 tablespoons butter, softened, divided
1/8 teaspoon ground nutmeg
1/4 cup light brown sugar
1/4 teaspoon ground cinnamon
1 rolled refrigerated pie crust (from a 15-ounce package)
4 small Granny Smith apples, peeled and cored

Directions:

1. Preheat oven to 375 degrees F.
2. In a small saucepan, combine the water, white sugar, vanilla, 1 tablespoon butter, and nutmeg over high heat.
3. Bring to a boil for 1 minute.
4. Set aside.
5. In a small bowl, combine the brown sugar, cinnamon, and remaining 1 tablespoon butter.
6. Mix well.
7. Unroll pastry and cut into quarters. Stuff each apple cavity with an equal amount of brown sugar mixture and place on a pastry quarter. Fold pastry up around apples and pinch ends together to completely enclose apples. Place dumplings seam-side down in an 8-inch square baking dish and pour sugar sauce over the top.
8. Bake 45 to 50 minutes, or until golden. Serve warm, drizzled with sugar glaze from bottom of baking dish.

Amish Chow Chow

Chow chow is a relish-like dish made of chopped pickles and a seasoned mustard sauce.

The Amish add garden vegetables in their version of chow chow which gives it a variety of wholesome flavors.

Ingredients:

1 cup chopped green tomatoes
1 cup chopped bell peppers
1 cup cabbage, chopped
1 whole cucumber, chopped
1 cup onions, chopped
2 qt. water
1/4 cup salt
1 cup carrots, chopped
1 cup green beans, chopped
2 tsp. mustard seed
2 tsp. celery seed
2 cup vinegar
2 cup sugar

Directions:

1. Soak the tomatoes, peppers, cucumbers and onions overnight in water and salt.
2. Drain.
3. Cook carrots and green beans for 10 minutes.
4. Drain.
5. Mix all ingredients.
6. Heat to a boil.
7. Pack in jars and seal.

Pennsylvania Dutch Beet Eggs

Ingredients:

2 (15 oz.) cans whole pickled beets, juice reserved
1 onion, chopped
1 cup white sugar
3/4 cup cider vinegar
1/2 tsp. salt
1 pinch ground black pepper
2 bay leaves
12 whole cloves

Directions:

1. Place eggs in saucepan and cover with water.
2. Bring to boil.
3. Cover, remove from heat, and let eggs sit in hot water for 10 to 12 minutes.
4. Remove from hot water, cool, and peel.
5. Place beets, onion, and peeled eggs in a non-reactive glass or plastic container. Set aside.
6. In a medium-size, non-reactive saucepan, combine sugar, 1 cup reserved beet juice, vinegar, salt, pepper, bay leaves, and cloves. Bring to a boil, lower heat, and simmer 5 minutes.
7. Pour hot liquid over beets and eggs.
8. Cover, and refrigerate 48 hours before using.

Amish Cole Slaw

Ingredients:

6 cups of grated cabbage
3/4 cup grated carrots
2 tbs. chopped onion
Dressing:
4 cups mayonnaise
1/4 cup mustard
1 1/8 cup sugar
2 tbs. pickle juice

Directions:

1. Combine vegetables.
2. Combine dressing ingredients and mix with vegetables.
3. Toss to combine all ingredients.
4. Best if chilled for 24 hours.
5. Serve and enjoy!

Amish Corn Soup with Rivels

Ingredients:

3 cups corn (fresh or canned)
2 qts. water
1 cup rich milk
1 1/3 cups flour
1 egg
3 tbsp. butter
1½ tsp. salt
parsley

Directions:

1. Cook corn in water for 10 minutes.
2. Make a batter by mixing egg, flour and milk together.
3. Pour batter through a colander, letting it drop into the boiling corn.
4. Add butter and salt.
5. Cook slowly in a covered pan for 3 minutes.
6. Garnish with chopped parsley.
7. Serve and enjoy!

Lancaster Amish Pretzels

Ingredients:

1¼ cup warm water (not too warm, but warmer than lukewarm)
1 tablespoon active dry yeast
¼ cup brown sugar
2 cup bread flour
2 cup self-rising flour
1 teaspoon vegetable or canola oil
½ cup baking soda
3 cups hot water (but not too hot to put hands in)
4 tablespoons butter, melted
rock salt

Directions:

1. In a large bowl or standing mixer, mix yeast and 1¼ cup warm water.
2. Let sit for 2 minutes.
3. Add brown sugar, bread flour, self-rising flour and vegetable oil to the yeast and mix to combine completely.
4. Knead on a lightly-floured surface to form a ball of dough.
5. Place in a greased bowl and cover with a cloth.
6. Let rise for 45 minutes, until double in size.
7. Preheat oven to 450° F.
8. Lightly grease a clean large flat surface like the counter or spray with cooking spray.
9. Dump the dough ball out onto the greased part of the counter.
10. Form a uniform rectangle and then cut the dough into 12 equal pieces.
11. To form the pretzels, pick up a piece of dough and roll and stretch it out into a long thin rope on the un-greased portion of your countertop.
12. The dough rope should be about the length of your arm and skinny.
13. Form in to a pretzel shape and attach the ends to itself.
14. Whisk together baking soda and hot water in a large bowl.
15. Get a clean dish towel, folded, and place it next to the bowl.
16. Dip the formed pretzel into the solution then blot the bottom side of the pretzel on the towel before placing on a greased cookie sheet or cookie sheet lined with a Silpat.
17. Whisk the water before each dip as the baking soda settles quickly. Bake for 5-10 minutes, until pretzels are a dark golden brown.
18. Brush with melted butter and sprinkle with rock salt.
19. To make cinnamon-sugar pretzels, dip the cooked pretzels completely in butter then coat in cinnamon sugar.
20. Best served fresh out of the oven.
21. Leftovers can be reheated in a 325° oven for about 4 minutes.

Authentic Amish Potato Salad

Potato Salad Ingredients:

4 slices bacon
½ cup chopped onion
½ cup chopped green pepper
¼ cup vinegar
1 teaspoon salt
3 eggs, hard-boiled
⅛ tsp. pepper
1 tsp. sugar
1 egg (not hard-boiled)
1 qt. potatoes, cooked and cubed (4 cups)
¼ cup grated raw carrot

Potato Salad Directions:

Dice bacon and pan fry.
Add chopped onion and green pepper.
Cook 3 minutes.
Add vinegar, salt, pepper, sugar and beaten egg.
Cook slightly.
Add potatoes, grated carrot and diced hard-cooked eggs.
Make dressing below and add to mixture.

Dressing Ingredients:

1 beaten egg
½ cup sugar
1 tbsp. flour
½ cup water
½ cup vinegar
2 tbsp. butter
½ tsp. salt
¼ tsp. pepper

Dressing Directions:

1. Combine in the order given, stirring after each addition.
2. Boil until thick.
3. Cool.
4. Add to the potato salad mixture.
5. Stir until well mixed.

Pennsylvania Dutch Meat Rolls

Also known as Boova Shenkel

Ingredients:

2½ lbs. beef
10 potatoes
2 tbs. butter
2 tbs. minced parsley
1 chopped onion
½ tsp. salt
½ cup milk
3 eggs
2½ cups flour
2 tsp. baking powder
1 tbs. shortening
1 tbs. butter

Directions:

1. Season the meat with salt and pepper.
2. Stew the meat for two hours.
3. Make the dough by mixing the flour, baking powder, salt and shortening.
4. Roll into a dozen circles 8 to 10 inches in diameter.
5. Steam the potatoes and then peel and sliced thin.
6. Put potatoes in a bowl and add salt and pepper, 2 tablespoons of butter, parsley and onions.
7. Beat the eggs into the mixture.
8. Put the mixture on the circles of dough.
9. Fold the circles over like a half moon and press edges together tightly.
10. Skim a couple of tablespoons of fat from the stew and set aside before dropping in the dough rolls.
11. Drop the dough rolls into the pot with the meat and stew water.
12. Cover tightly and cook for 30 minutes.
13. Put the skimmed fat from the stew in a frying pan.
14. Add 1 tablespoon of butter.
15. Brown small cubes of hard bread.
16. Stir in a half cup of milk.
17. Stir to make a milk sauce. Pour the milk sauce over the rolls when serving.

Pennsylvania Dutch Pot Pie

Ingredients

4-5 chicken breasts or thighs
1 cup chopped onion
1 tsp. celery seed
3 large potatoes, peeled and cut into bite sized chunks
4 carrots, peeled and sliced into 1/4 inch slices
1/2 tsp. garlic powder
2 tbsp. chopped fresh parsley or dried parsley flakes
5 chicken bouillon cubes
2 1/2 cup flour
3/4 stick butter, softened
1/3 cup milk
salt and pepper to taste
1 egg

Stock Directions:

1. Fill a large Dutch oven with about 2 quarts of water.
2. Add the chopped onion, celery seed, garlic powder, parsley, bouillon cubes and chicken.
3. Bring to a boil, cover with lid, and then turn down to simmer for about an hour, or until chicken can be easily removed from the bones.
4. Remove chicken from the pot, reserving all of the stock.
5. Turn off the burner until after the noodles are made (recipe follows).
6. Remove chicken from bones and cut into small chunks and set aside.

Noodle Directions:

1. Pour flour into a mixing bowl and add softened butter and egg.
2. Add about ½ teaspoon of salt and 1/4 teaspoon pepper (or to taste). Begin mixing using your hands, and then add milk.
3. Completely mix dough with your hands until you reach desired consistency (you may need to add a little flour or a little more milk, depending...dough should not be sticky to the touch.
4. If too sticky, add a little flour until just right.
5. Flour your surface, then roll out dough with rolling pin to about 1/4 inch thick. Using a sharp knife, cut slices the entire way across, and then the other direction, to form square noodles about 1-1/2" square.

6. Bring stock to a rolling boil, add potatoes and carrots, and a handful of the noodles at a time. Stir soup after each addition of noodles to help keep them from sticking together.
7. Cover again with lid, and let cook for about a half hour to 45 minutes, or until noodles are cooked completely through and the vegetables are done.
8. When all is finished, add the chicken once again, to heat through, and serve.
9. The broth will thicken up a little after you add your noodles.

Browned Butter Noodles

Ingredients:

1 (12 oz.) package egg noodles
½ cup butter

Directions:

1. Cook noodles according to package directions.
2. Melt the butter in a saucepan.
3. Once the butter is melted stir and watch.
4. The butter will turn golden and then brown.
5. Wait until the butter has turned medium to dark brown and take it off the heat.
6. Drain noodles and pour the butter over them.
7. The butter will sizzle when it hits the noodles.
8. There will be little brown flecks on the noodles.

Amish Corn Fritters

Ingredients:

4 lg. ears corn
2 large eggs, beaten
3/4 cup flour, sifted
3/4 tsp. salt
1/4 tsp. pepper
1 tsp. baking powder

Directions:

1. Cut the corn kernels from cobb into a bowl.
2. With the back of the knife, scrape the cobs to extract the juice from the cobs.
3. Scrape the pulp on the cob into the bowl.
4. Combine corn and eggs.
5. Sift the flour, salt, pepper and baking powder together in a separate bowl.
6. Add the flour mixture to the corn and egg mixture.
7. Drop tablespoons of the corn batter into a 1 inch of melted shortening.
8. Brown until golden on both sides, turning once.
9. Lay out on paper towels to drain.
10. Serve and enjoy!

Schnitz Un Gnepp

Schnitz Ingredients:

2 lb. smoked ham
2 tbsp. brown sugar
2 cups dried sweet apples
1 cups raisins
2 qt. ham broth

Gnepp Ingredients:

2 1/2 Cup flour
4 tsp. baking powder
1/2 tsp. salt
1 egg, beaten
2 Tbsp. butter
3/4 Cup milk

Schnitz Directions:

1. Cook ham, apples, and raisins slowly in a roaster for 2 plus hours in about a quart of water.
2. Add brown sugar and cook 1 hour longer. Add more water as needed (about ½ quart)
3. When the ham is finished cooking transfer ham broth, apples, and raisins to a large cooking pot and add another quart of ham broth.
4. Bring the broth to a boil

Gnepp Directions:

1. In another bowl mixed together flour, baking powder, and salt.
2. Stir in beaten egg and melted butter
3. Add enough milk to make a moderately stiff batter.
4. Drop with a spoon into boiling ham broth.
5. Use a tablespoon for small dough balls or 1/4 cup for larger balls.
6. Cover the pot tightly and cook without lifting the lid for 20 minutes. (Lifting the lid prevents the dough from getting as fluffy)
7. Serve and enjoy!

Pennsylvania Dutch Sauerbraten

Ingredients:

4 lb. roast of top round of beef
1 cup dry red wine
3/4 cup wine vinegar
1½ cup water
1 med. onion, sliced thin
1 tsp. salt
8 whole black peppercorns, broken
4 whole cloves
2 bay leaves
1/4 tsp. ground ginger
3 tbsp. vegetable shortening
1/2 cup chopped onions
1/2 cup diced carrots
1/2 cup chopped celery
3 T. flour
2/3 cup water

Directions:

1. In a 2-quart saucepan, combine the wine, vinegar, water, onions, salt, and spices.
2. Bring to a boil.
3. Remove from the heat and cool to room temperature.
4. Put the beef in a 1-gallon crockpot or a stainless steel pot.
5. Choose a pot which is not much larger than the roast but leaves enough room for the marinade.
6. Pour the marinade over the roast, and refrigerate for 3 days.
7. Turn the meat twice each day.
8. When ready to cook the sauerbraten, remove it from the marinade and pat dry with paper towels.
9. train the marinade and save it, but discard the onions and spices.
10. Melt the shortening in a 3-quart saucepot.
11. Brown the sauerbraten on all sides.
12. Remove the meat and sauté the onions, carrots and celery until the onions are clear.
13. Add the flour and stir until golden brown.
14. Gradually add the marinade and water, and stir until it comes to a boil.
15. Add the meat.
16. Cover and simmer for 1 hour and 15 minutes (45 minutes if you desire the beef to be pink in the center).
17. Serve and enjoy!

Mennonite Ham Loaf

Loaf Ingredients:

1 lb. fresh ground turkey
1 lb. ham, ground
1 cup breadcrumbs
1 egg
1 teaspoon salt
1/8 teaspoon pepper
3/4 cup milk

Sauce Ingredients:

2/3 cup brown sugar
1 teaspoon dry mustard
1/2 cup water
1/4 cup vinegar

Directions:

1. Grind meat if necessary.
2. Mix ground meats, breadcrumbs, egg, salt, pepper and milk together.
3. Shape into a loaf.
4. Bake at 350 degrees F. for one hour.
5. For the sauce, mix the brown sugar, dry mustard, water and vinegar together.
6. Pour sauce over loaf.
7. Continue to bake for another hour.
8. Serve and enjoy!

Pennsylvania Dutch Potato Filling

Ingredients:

10 pounds potatoes, peeled and cut into 1 inch cubes
2 cups butter, divided
3 onions, diced
1 bunch celery, diced
1 1/2 cups milk, divided
3 tbs. seasoned salt, divided
1 (1 1/4 lb.) loaf of white bread, torn into pieces, divided

Directions:

1. Place the potato cubes into a large pot and cover with salted water. Bring to a boil over high heat, then reduce heat to medium-low, cover, and simmer until tender, about 25 minutes.
2. Drain and allow to steam dry for a minute or two.
3. Melt 1/2 cup of butter in a large skillet over medium heat, and cook and stir the onions and celery until they are reduced and browned, about 30 minutes.
4. Preheat oven to 350 degrees F.
5. Grease 2 glass baking dishes, each 9 x 13 inches.
6. Place another 1/2 cup of butter into the bowl of a standing mixer, and add the cooked potatoes.
7. Start the mixer on Low setting.
8. While mixer is running, pour in 1 cup of milk, and add 1 tablespoon of seasoned salt and 4 slices of torn bread.
9. Mix those ingredients briefly into the mixture, and pour in 1/2 cup of milk and 4 more bread slices.
10. Mix, and then mix in 2 more bread slices.
11. After the last 2 bread slices have been roughly incorporated, place another 1/2 cup of butter, 1 tablespoon of seasoned salt, all the onions, celery, and butter from the skillet, and 4 more slices of bread into the mixer bowl.
12. Mix to incorporate, and finally mix in 2 to 4 additional torn bread slices.
13. Allow the mixer to run until the dressing is the desired consistency.
14. Place half the dressing into each prepared baking dish, and top the dressing with the remaining 1/2 cup of butter, cut into thin slices and scattered over the top.
15. Sprinkle remaining 1 tablespoon of seasoned salt evenly over the top of the dishes.
16. Cover the dishes with aluminum foil.
17. Bake in the preheated oven until the dressing is browned, about 1 hour.
18. Serve and enjoy!

Amish Friendship Bread

Ingredients

1 cup Amish Friendship Bread Starter (recipe below)
3 eggs
1 cup oil
½ cup milk
1 cup sugar
½ teaspoon vanilla
2 tsp. cinnamon
1½ teaspoon baking powder
½ teaspoon salt
½ teaspoon baking soda
2 cups flour
1-2 small boxes instant pudding (any flavor)
1 cup nuts, chopped (optional)
1 cup raisins (optional)

Directions:

1. Preheat oven to 325° F.
2. In a mixer or bowl, mix together the ingredients in the order listed.
3. Grease two large loaf pans.
4. Dust the greased pans with a mixture of ½ cup sugar and ½ teaspoon cinnamon.
5. Pour the batter evenly into the loaf pans and sprinkle the remaining cinnamon-sugar mixture on the top.
6. Bake for one hour or until the bread loosens evenly from the sides and a toothpick inserted in the center of the bread comes out clean.
7. Serve and enjoy!

Amish Friendship Bread Starter

Ingredients:

1 (0.25 oz.) package active dry yeast
¼ cup warm water
1 cup all-purpose flour
1 cup white sugar
1 cup milk

Directions:

1. In a small bowl, dissolve yeast in water.
2. Let stand 10 minutes.
3. In a 2 quart glass, plastic or ceramic container, combine 1 cup flour and 1 cup sugar.
4. Mix thoroughly with a whisk or fork.
5. Slowly stir in 1 cup milk and dissolved yeast mixture.
6. Cover loosely and let stand at room temperature until bubbly.
7. This is day 1 of the 10 day cycle.
8. For the next 10 days follow the directions below.
9. The starter should be left at room temperature.
10. Drape loosely with dish towel or plastic wrap.
11. Do not use metal utensils or bowls.
12. If using a sealed Ziploc bag, let the air out if the bag gets too puffy.

Starter 10 Day Cycle:

Day 1: Do nothing.
Day 2: Mash the bag.
Day 3: Mash the bag.
Day 4: Mash the bag.
Day 5: Mash the bag.
Day 6: Add to the bag: 1 cup flour, 1 cup sugar, 1 cup milk. Mash the bag.
Day 7: Mash the bag.
Day 8: Mash the bag.
Day 9: Mash the bag.
Day 10: Follow the directions below:

1. Pour the entire bag into a nonmetal bowl.
2. Add 1½ cup flour, 1½ cup sugar, 1½ cup milk.
3. Measure out equal portions of 1 cup each into 4 1-gallon Ziploc bags.

Note: Your starter will yield between 4-7 portions depending on how active your starter has been. If you yield more portions than needed, freeze the extra portions.

Amish Potato Rolls

Ingredients:

2 eggs
1/3 cup sugar
1 1/2 tsp. salt
6 tbs. butter
1 cup mashed potatoes
2 1/2 tsp. instant yeast
3/4 cup milk
4 1/4 cups all-purpose flour

Directions:

1. In a mixing bowl, combine all of the ingredients, and mix until the dough starts to leave the sides of the bowl.
2. Transfer the dough to a lightly greased or floured surface, and knead it for 6 to 8 minutes, or until it's smooth and shiny.
3. Place the dough in a lightly greased bowl, turn to coat.
4. Cover the bowl with plastic wrap and let the dough rise until it has doubled in bulk (about 90 minutes).
5. Divide the dough into 16 equal pieces.
6. Gently roll the dough pieces in to round balls.
7. Place the dough balls on a parchment-lined or lightly greased baking sheet, leaving about 2 inches between them.
8. Cover the pan with lightly greased plastic wrap, and allow the rolls to rise for about 2 hours until they are puffy.
9. Bake the rolls in a preheated 350 degree F oven for 20 to 25 minutes until golden brown.
10. Brush with melted butter, if desired.
11. Serve and enjoy!.

Snickerdoodles

Ingredients:

1 cup butter softened
1 1/2 cup sugar
2 eggs
2¾ cups flour
2 tsp. cream of tartar
1 teaspoon baking soda
½ teaspoon salt

Directions:

1. Preheat the oven to 400 degrees F.
2. Cream the butter, sugar, and eggs.
3. Stir in the dry ingredients.
4. Chill the dough for at least 20 minutes
5. Roll the dough into balls the size of walnuts.
6. Sift together 2 tablespoons of sugar and 2 tablespoons cinnamon
7. Roll the balls the mixture.
8. Place the balls on an ungreased baking sheet about 2 inches apart.
9. Bake for 8-10 minutes.
10. Cool on a wire cookie rack.
11. Serve and enjoy!

Amish Gingersnaps Cookies

Ingredients:

3/4 cup butter
1 cup sugar
1 egg
1/4 cup molasses
2 cups flour
2 tsp. baking soda
1/4 tsp. salt
1 tsp. cinnamon
1 tsp. cloves
1 tsp. ginger

Directions:

1. In a mixing bowl, cream the butter and sugar.
2. Add eggs and molasses.
3. Beat well.
4. Sift together the dry ingredients.
5. Gradually add to creamed mixture.
6. Mix well.
7. Chill the dough.
8. Roll into balls and dip in sugar.
9. Bake at 375 degrees F. for 10 minutes or until set and surface cracks.
10. Cool on a wire rack.
11. Serve and enjoy!

Shoofly Pie

Ingredients:

Bottom Part

3/4 cup dark molasses (sorghum or dark Karo)
3/4 cup boiling water
1/2 tsp. baking soda

Ingredients for Top Part:

1 1/2 cups flour
1/4 cup shortening or 1/4 cup butter
1/2 cup brown sugar
1 (9") pastry dough

Directions:

1. Dissolve baking soda in hot water.
2. Add molasses.
3. Combine sugar and flour and rub in shortening to make crumbs.
4. Pour 1/3 of the liquid into an unbaked crust.
5. Add 1/3 of the crumb mixture.
6. Continue alternating layers, ending with crumbs on top.
7. Bake at 375 degrees F. for approximately 35 minutes.
8. Cool on a wire rack.
9. Serve and enjoy!

Whoopie pie

Cookie Dough Ingredients:

2 cup all-purpose flour
1 cup sugar
¾ cup milk
½ cup unsweetened cocoa
6 tbsp. butter or margarine
1 tsp. baking soda
1 tsp. vanilla extract
¼ tsp. salt
1 large egg

Marshmallow Cream Filling Ingredients:

6 tbsp. butter or margarine
1 cup confectioners' sugar
1 jar marshmallow cream
1 tsp. vanilla extract

Directions:

1. Preheat oven to 350 degrees F.
2. Grease 2 large cookie sheets.
3. Prepare the cookie dough by combining all the cookie ingredients in a large bowl and mixing until smooth.
4. Drop dough by heaping tablespoons about 2 inches apart on a prepared cookie sheet. There should be 24 cookies. Twelve on each cookie sheet.
5. Bake 12 to 14 minutes, rotating sheets between upper and lower racks halfway through baking, until puffy and toothpick inserted in center comes out clean.
6. With a wide spatula, transfer cookies to wire racks to cool.
7. Prepare marshmallow cream: First beat butter until smooth with a mixer.
8. Reduce speed to low and gradually beat in confectioners' sugar.
9. Beat in marshmallow cream and vanilla until smooth.
10. Spread 1 rounded tablespoon filling on flat side of 12 of the cookies.
11. Top with remaining half of cookies.
12. Serve and enjoy!

The End

About the Author

Laura Sommers is a loving wife and mother who lives in Baltimore County, Maryland and has a passion for all things domestic especially when it comes to saving money. She has a profitable eBay business and is a couponing addict. She challenges herself to write books that are enriching, enjoyable, and often unconventional.

Other books by Laura Sommers

Recipes for the Zombie Apocalypse Series

Recipes for the Zombie Apocalypse Vol. 1

Okay, so you prep and prep for the end of days and when the zombie apocalypse finally happens, what are you going to do? You need recipes for all your shelf stable foods. This book will show the survivalist how to cook lots of delicious meals with foods straight from your pantry.

Recipes for the Zombie Apocalypse Vol. 2

Recipes for the Zombie Apocalypse Volume 2 cookbook is full of mouth-watering recipes using only foraged foods and items from your pantry. No refrigerated items. Enjoy!

Homesteading Cookbooks

Egg Recipes for People with Backyard Chickens

If you have backyard Chickens, I'm sure that you have come across the dilemma of having more eggs than you know what to do with! I have compiled a list of great egg recipes so that you can start to fulfill your dream of living off the land (at least partially) and know that you are feeding your family without good wholesome eggs that come from your own chickens

Regional & Holiday Cookbooks

Traditional Cajun and Creole Recipes From New Orleans

What do you think of when you think of New Orleans? If you are like me, you think of food! New Orleans, Louisiana is known for a lot of things: Mardi Gras, Jazz Festivals, Riverboats, Bourbon Street and lot of rich, flavorful food dishes that are specific to just that one city. There is both Creole and Cajun style dishes and I like them both. After spending over three years in New Orleans and taking several cooking classes on the cuisine I have written this recipe book with some of my favorite dishes. I hope that you enjoy!

Best Traditional Irish Recipes for St. Patrick's Day

All your favorite Irish recipes to cook in your own kitchen for St. Patrick's Day! Who needs to travel to the Emerald Isle for traditional Irish Dishes. This recipe book has all your favorites straight from Ireland to help you celebrate the St. Patrick's Day holiday such as corned beef and cabbage, Irish stew, soda bread and much much more!

Super Awesome Traditional Maryland Recipes

"Maryland is for Crabs." But not just any crab. Specifically the Chesapeake Blue Crab which is indigenous to the Chesapeake Bay.

This recipe book is not all seafood but everything has been made with the spirit of Maryland cuisine in mind. There are recipes for cooking crab cakes, soft shell crabs, crab soup, boardwalk fries and much, much more! I hope that you enjoy!

Simple Cheap One Dish Meals Series

Super Awesome Inexpensive Casserole Recipes

Casseroles are the perfect idea for hard working families on a budget. They are quick, easy, inexpensive and delicious! They can be made ahead of time and then frozen or reheated. They are perfect for pot lucks, parties, work team events, family reunions, barbecues, holidays and picnics!

Super Awesome Inexpensive Casserole Recipes Vol. 2

If you loved my first book on casserole recipes, or even if you haven't read that book, you are in for a treat. While the first book focused on the more traditional casserole dishes, this book looks at cooking the less trendy or lesser known one dish ideas.

Low Carb Recipe Book Series

Inexpensive Low Carb Recipes

The low carb diet may help you lose weight but it can be expensive. Here are a list of low carbohydrate recipes that are inexpensive to make.

Low Carb Chicken Recipes on The Grill

Watching your carbohydrates can be easy when you have a cook book like this full of delicious tasty chicken on the grill recipes.

Low Carb Chicken Recipes on the Stove Top

Watching your carbohydrates can be easy when you have a cook book like this full of delicious tasty chicken from the stove top recipes. This cookbook shows you how to cook many different types of chicken dishes on the stovetop including chicken piccata, chicken stroganoff and chicken marsala.

Gourmet Low Carb Fish & Seafood Recipes

Watching your carbohydrates can be easy when you have a cook book like this full of delicious tasty seafood and fish recipes. This cookbook shows you how to cook many different types of seafood and fish including shrimp, snapper, oysters, clams, halibut, tuna, catfish, crab tilapia, lobster and scallops.

Low Carb Steak and Beef Recipes On The Grill

Watching your carbohydrates can be easy when you have a cook book like this full of delicious tasty steak and beef on the grill recipes. This cookbook shows you how to cook many different types of steak dishes on the grill including Shish Kabob Steak, Steak Royal, Teriyaki Beef, Grilled Meat Loaf, Cajun Stuffed Steak and Skewered Beef with Peanut Sauce to name a few.

Super Awesome Farm Fresh Pork Chop Recipes

Pork Chops are so versatile! They can be baked, fried, stuffed and grilled! They are the perfect food for a Summer cookout and barbeque! They can be savory, smoky, tangy or sweet! They are also low carb for those of us who are looking for a healthy low carbohydrate option!

Sugar Free and Diabetic Cookbooks

Awesome Sugar Free Diabetic Recipes

Are you on a diabetic meal plan? Are you carb conscious and looking for a low sugar or sugar free option in order to have your pie and eat it too? Here are all your favorite pie recipes and made low carb and diabetic friendly versions. And less sugar and less carbs means low calorie so they are also great for those of us trying to lose weight. Because everyone should be able to enjoy a good slice of pie!

Smoothie Recipe Books

Totally Bare Green Smoothie Recipes

If you are looking for smoothie recipes, especially green smoothie recipes, then you are probably looking for recipes that are the healthiest that you can get.
That is why drinking green smoothies that adhere to the raw and vegan diet are arguably the most nutritious and beneficial to a healthy diet.
Here is a list of delicious green smoothie recipes that are totally Raw and totally Vegan. In other words, TOTALLY BARE! Enjoy!

Potato Recipe Books

Super Awesome Potato Recipes Vol. 1

Potatoes are popular the world over and available year round. They are a staple food because they are so versatile. They are the number one crop in the world. They can be mashed, baked, roasted, fried, boiled or whipped. They can be added to soups, served on the side or eaten as a main dish.

With that in mind, I have started this series of recipe books featuring the potato. This is Volume One. I hope that you enjoy!

Vegan Recipe Books

Super Slimming Vegan Soup Recipes!

Whether you like creamy soup, spicy soup, broth soup or gazpacho soup finding low calorie vegan soups can be a challenge when you are trying to lose weight and are on a diet. This collection of super slimming, super easy and super delicious recipes has something for everyone's vegan pallet. If you are losing weight and looking for recipes that are made with healthy low calorie foods such as fruits and vegetables, then look no further! This recipe book contains a list of the best recipes for the vegan weight watcher to help you slim down, slenderize and lose weight. They are super quick, super easy, super delicious and super slimming!

Summer Fun Recipe Books

Super Summer Barbecue Picnic Salad Recipes

Summer is the best time for barbecues, family picnics, class reunions, pool parties. Deck parties, cookouts and all other get togethers. There's Memorial Day, Bastille Day, Independence Day (4th of July) and Labor Day! Not to mention all the baseball games and soccer games. Who doesn't love to fire up the grill and sit back and relax with good food and mouth-watering dishes? With every BBQ or party you need side dishes and salads are a great choice. Recipes included are macaroni salad, coleslaw, potato salad, fruit salad and ambrosia salad.

Easy to Make Party Dip Recipes!

What's a party without great party dip! Whatever kind of dip you want: chip dip, veggie dip, spicy, sweet or tangy, you don't want it to be complicated. You want to fix it quick and get down to the partying! Whatever your preference: zesty, tasty, savory. Hot or cold when you realize how tasty these quick and simple recipes are, you will never want to serve store bought dips ever again!

Popcorn Lovers Recipe Book

Popcorn is an inexpensive cheap snack that is extremely versatile when it comes to adding flavoring. It can be sweet, spicy or savory. You can add cheese, butter, spices, chocolate or salt. Here is a collection of recipes for the snack chef to make that are inexpensive and delicious.

Super Awesome Barbecue Sauce, Spice And Rub Recipes For The Grill Or Smoker

Barbecue is big all over the southern United States but there are versions of barbecue all over the world! From Korea to Jamaica there are countless varieties of sauces, rubs and spices.

This cook book is full of mouthwatering recipes for your BBQ meals. If you are looking for the perfect sauce, rub or spice this book has it. Whether it is for Memorial Day, Bastille Day, Independence Day, 4th of July, Labor Day, Grilling by the pool, on the beach in the Summertime, for a Summer picnic, cookout, family reunion or get together a Pool Party, Fiesta or Backyard Barbeque this recipe book has it.

May all of your meals be a banquet
with good friends and good food.

Made in the USA
Lexington, KY
02 August 2016